Writing Effective
REPORT CARD
Comments

by
Susan Shafer

SCHOLASTIC
PROFESSIONAL BOOKS

NEW YORK • TORONTO • LONDON • AUCKLAND • SYDNEY

DEDICATION
To Marilyn

ACKNOWLEDGMENTS
My thanks to the teachers and consultants who contributed
their time and thoughts to this book, especially Adam Berkin,
Miriam Epland, Adele Fiderer, Min Hong, Gloria Hoyos,
Jane Fowler, Mary Gallivan, Kathy Lake, Fran McNulty,
Yvonne Sui Runyan, Peggy Scott, Leslie Serling, Penny Strube,
Kathy Sholtys, Suzanne Houghton Varney, and Valerie Williams.

The report card excerpt on page 11 is reproduced from the archives of the New York City Board of Education:
New York City Board of Education Archives, Millbank Memorial Library, Teachers College, Columbia University.

Cover design by Vincent Ceci and Jaime Lucero
Interior design by Solutions by Design, Inc.

ISBN 0-590-06882-2

Table of Contents

Introduction

"A report card," says Penny Strube, a fifth-grade teacher in Hannibal, Missouri, *"is a keepsake for the whole family. It's a piece of memorabilia that a child may keep for a lifetime. So, when I write comments on my students' report cards, I compose very carefully, basing my statements on careful observation of the child's work. I know that in future years those kids may one day reread what I said about them when they were students in my class. It's a big responsibility, and I try to be positive and encouraging."*

This is part of a conversation I had with *one* teacher, which grew into conversations with *many* teachers across the country, on how to make comments we teachers write on students' report cards more meaningful and helpful to the child and the child's family.

Report card comments have always been an interest of mine. During the twenty years I worked as an elementary school teacher, I often wished that we teachers had more opportunities to share ideas on how to write the best narratives possible. While I was confident that the report cards I wrote were clear, straightforward, and informative, I wished that I had further chances to discuss with my colleagues our philosophies about report card writing and our approaches to and systems for collecting data. By sharing ideas, we would grow as professionals and our improved narratives would help students grow as learners.

Questioning Begins

Some months ago I plunged into the research that I had wanted to undertake for so long. Now an educational writer and consultant, I started by phoning teacher friends and colleagues, asking them to discuss with me the basic tenets and practical assessment systems that guide them as they prepare report cards.

My plan was to write a book that would give teachers the tools to communicate more effectively with parents. I hoped to make it easier for teachers to create narratives that are clear and *constructive*—in the fullest sense of that word. I wanted to help teachers write comments that would build kids' confidence and improve their learning.

Phone Calls Galore

"Tell me about your philosophy of writing report card comments," I began, after chatting informally with each teacher. (Their response? Make it positive.) "What do you hope report cards will accomplish?" I also asked. "Who are you trying to reach?"

Teachers were eager to discuss these questions and were happy to share their thoughts and practices. Many even wrote letters and sent me sample narratives to illustrate their points. The interviews were so spirited and information-packed that I began to take notes.

Distributed Questionnaire

Soon I formalized my work even more. I created a questionnaire which I sent to eight outstanding teachers. (They teach various grades, from grade 1 through grade 5, and some have taught preschool or grade 6 and higher in the past. One taught a range of grades from K—12 and is currently an associate professor in a university.)

Moms and Dads Queried

I also wanted *parents'* views about narratives. In time, I contacted parents of my former students, friends of relatives, and neighbors.

Purpose

The purpose of *Writing Effective Report Card Comments* is to help you:

☞ Write report card comments with clarity and ease.

☞ Share information that encourages parents' support of their children's learning.

☞ Make the report card writing process more efficient.

The book describes the four most important elements of effective narratives and offers tips and actual examples of report card comments that work.

Chapter 1

Report Cards in the Assessment Process

Assessment Is Ongoing

From the moment students enter your classroom in the morning till long after they leave at the end of the day, you are evaluating their progress, both formally and informally. Assessment is often so much a natural part of what we teachers do that we're hardly aware we're doing it. Yet assessment is vital in helping us promote students' growth as learners, in informing us about our own teaching, and in reporting students' progress to parents. Let's look at the ways in which all of these things come into play in one teacher's classroom.

After lunch, the students in a fourth-grade class gather for a writing workshop mini-lesson. The teacher starts by demonstrating for the group how to use dialogue to write a "catchy lead." After the discussion, the children return to their desks to experiment with leads for their own stories (they have learned several techniques so far this month). Before long, the teacher notices 11-year-old Shawn sitting dejectedly at his desk, crossing out some of his sentences, crumbling up his paper.

"What's wrong, Shawn?" the teacher asks.

"My leads are crummy," he says. "I've tried 'dialogue.' I've tried 'surprise statements.' But nothing sounds good enough to get my friends to read on. I'm stuck."

The teacher offers a suggestion. "Have you tried 'flashback'?" she asks. Shawn's face brightens, his body relaxes, and he goes back to writing with new energy.

Pleased, the teacher walks away, making a quick note to herself on a sticky paper: "January 4—Shawn struggling with leads." She drops the note into her folder for Shawn and makes a mental note to observe his progress in this area as the weeks go on. To see how he is coming along today, she will stop at the boy's desk again later in the writing workshop. She may even include a comment on his next report card: "Shawn is working on finding good leads for his stories."

The teacher jots down one more note, this one to herself: "Plan new lesson on leads. Ask kids to bring in books from home that have a lead that they like."

Later that month, when the teacher and Shawn's mother meet during a parent-teacher conference, they will look over Shawn's report card and portfolio and talk, in part, about Shawn's progress in this area.

This is just one example of how we teachers are involved in assessing our students on an ongoing basis—all day long, all year long.

Select From a Wide Range of Tools

There are so many assessment tools available to us as teachers—including observation, anecdotal records, conferences, portfolios, rubrics, checklists, student self-evaluation, and tests, to name just a few—that we generally select a few that are appropriate. How do we decide which assessment tools we will use? We base our decisions on:

☞ the grade level we teach. For example, a lower grade teacher may use a reading readiness checklist while an upper grade teacher may study children's daily reading logs.

☞ the subject we teach. For example, to assess math we may listen to a child's explanation of how he solved a problem, and to assess social studies we may read his written response to the question "Would you have liked to live in Colonial times?"

☞ school or district mandates

No matter what the grade or subject, or whether we assess formally or informally, most of us *are* required to write report cards. Report cards can serve some useful purposes. Let's take a look at what those are.

Why Use Report Cards?

Build Home-School Connections

Many families use the report card as an occasion to sit down together to talk about the child's progress. Gathered at the kitchen table or seated on the living room couch, parents and children often read the grades and comments together, celebrating the children's successes or making plans to improve weaker areas.

Document Growth Through Childhood

Many parents save their children's report cards from preschool to high school, storing them in family albums or in shoe boxes in the attic. As years go on and children become teenagers or young adults, families often take out the stacks of report cards, treasuring them as warm reminders of the child's growing-up years. Along with photographs, report cards document a child's development through time ("Look at Bernie's second-grade report card. He was even good in math back then!").

Inform Families About Children's Learning

A report card summarizes for the family the salient aspects of the child's progress. It indicates for the child and parents the strengths of that student, both academically (_____ 's written stories are imaginative and well organized) and socially (_____ shows leadership skills in his social studies group).

Report cards may also bring to the parents' attention areas in which the child needs extra help (_____ could use extra practice with multiplication by 4 and 5) and may include suggestions for ways parents can assist their child at home (Perhaps you can read to her for fifteen minutes every night). Report cards, then, are a way to increase dialogue between home and school.

Help Children Grow as Learners

Effective report cards can motivate children to set higher goals. For example, a child who has a ready grasp of science principles about electricity may be encouraged—through the report card as well as other forms of communication—to attain more challenging levels of achievement. When a child reads about herself: _____ excels in science. I would enjoy seeing her create an original science project on circuits and demonstrate it for the class, she will have a concrete suggestion that propels her to stretch her abilities. Report cards can raise a child's performance or suggest new goals not considered initially by the child or the family.

Reach Shy, Quieter Children

Those children in class who are shy and less vocal may demand less of the teacher's in-class attention than children who are more outgoing. (That does not mean that the teacher does not recognize *each* child and the range of his or her capabilities, of course.) But the report card—particularly through the written comment—can become a vehicle through which the teacher reminds the shy child that he or she is appreciated.

Recognize Each Child's Unique Qualities

Some elementary school principals add to teachers' comments by writing comments of their own. *(Michael—I'm glad to see that your attendance this semester has improved. Keep up the good work! —Dr. Williams)*. This makes all children—and parents—feel special.

Report cards, then, serve many useful purposes.

Changing Nature of Report Cards

Perhaps you or other teachers in your school have participated in a district-wide committee to revise your district's report cards. Committees like these are becoming increasingly common because teachers have found that the nature of teaching—and therefore, the nature of assessment—has changed during the last several years.

Pressure for Revision

As recently as fifteen years ago, educators sometimes presented subjects such as spelling, grammar, and composition as a set of isolated skills. Teachers assessed students' knowledge mainly through tests and reported children's progress by means of grades or numbers. But with the current emphasis on integrating subject areas through literature-based instruction, theme studies, writing process, problem solving, critical thinking, and collaborative learning, teachers today are likely to use alternative means of assessment—such as portfolios, performance assessments, conferences, and observations—to capture the full range of learning activities in the classroom.

Yet report cards do not always reflect these new methods and views of learning. As a result, many teachers are urging their districts to find ways to revise report card formats to create greater harmony between current approaches to instruction and reporting.

Comeback for Narratives

As far back as the early part of the twentieth century, teachers reported student progress through narratives. But with the passage in 1918 of compulsory attendance laws (and with their enforcement by 1930), larger numbers of students attended school and teachers' classrooms were crowded with learners (Guskey, 1996). When it came time to report to parents, teachers still wrote narratives but it was no longer efficient to do so.

As years went by, teachers gradually shifted to checklists to save time, especially with older students. Ironically, while report cards today contain checklists and grades, there is a shift away from grades and marks back to narratives again. In many school districts still using traditional report cards, teachers are supplementing the cards with written self-evaluations from students, narrative evaluations, and other data.

A LOOK BACK IN TIME: Did You Know?

In 1931:

☞ About 6% of report cards during the early 1930s included a section on health education. It advised young children to consume each of these daily:

> 1 pint to 1 quart milk
>
> a glass of water before breakfast
>
> 1 cooked cereal, fruit
>
> a green or leafy vegetable

☞ A few cities distributed color-coded report cards, indicating at a glance the overall quality of a child's work in school: blue meant excellent work, brown meant very good, and so forth. Presumably, privacy was not highly valued, as children would quickly know their teacher's view of their own as well as classmates' work by the color of the card!

☞ A city in the West included space on their report cards for grades in these areas of children's home responsibilities: canning, care of stock, care of poultry, dusting, general farmwork, ironing, and milking.

Attendance and Punctuality

	Oct. 31	Dec. 15	Jan. 31
	Mar. 15	May 15	Jun. 30
ABSENT			
LATE			

P.S. _____   Borough _____

Board of Education
City of New York

———

REPORT CARD

———

Term beginning _____

Name _____

Class _____   Room _____

Teacher _____

First Report
In view of this pupil's ability, he (she)
1. Is doing very well   _____
2. Is doing satisfactory work   _____
3. Could do better   _____
4. Shows little effort   _____
I have read this report
   Parent's Signature_____

Second Report
In view of this pupil's ability, he (she)
1. Is doing very well   _____
2. Is doing satisfactory work   _____
3. Could do better   _____
4. Shows little effort   _____
I have read this report
   Parent's Signature_____

Second Report
In view of this pupil's ability, he (she)
1. Is doing very well   _____
2. Is doing satisfactory work   _____
3. Could do better   _____
4. Shows little effort   _____
I have read this report
   Parent's Signature_____

   Class nest term_____

TO PARENTS:

   The school is trying to aid the growth of your child in scholarship, in health habits and in character. To get the best results inside and outside school, your help is needed.

   The principal and the teacher will be pleased to talk matters over with you.

NAME_____

In the development of these traits, the home shares responsibility with the school.

TRAINING IN PERSONALITY	Oct. 31	Dec. 15	Jan. 31
Desirable Traits	Mar. 15	May 15	Jun. 30
1. Works and plays well with others			
2. Completes work			
3. Is generally careful			
4. Respects the rights of others			
5. Practices good health habits			
6. Speaks clearly			

Scholarship	Oct. 31	Dec. 15	Jan. 31
	Mar. 15	May 15	Jun. 30
Reading			
Literature			
Composition			
Arithmetic			
Geography			
History and Civics			
Penmanship			
Health Education			
Sewing or Construction			
Art			
Music			
Nature			

MEANING OF RATINGS

S—Satisfactory   U—Unsatisfactory

I—Improvement is shown

A—Excellent   B—Good

C—Passable   D—Failing

When per cent. ratings are used, _____% is the passing rating, except in spelling where _____% is required.

NEEDED IMPROVEMENT

Reading	Second Period	Third Period

An excerpt from a 1940 New York City report card (above) *and one from a 1996 Shaker Heights, Ohio, report card* (pages 13, 14) *shows how educators have moved toward a more descriptive and integrated approach to curriculum and evaluation.*

Shaker Heights Schools

Shaker Heights, Ohio 44120-2599

EDUCATIONAL REPORT

STUDENT _____

TEACHER _____

ABSENT   I _____   II _____   III _____

TARDY   I _____   II _____   III _____

CONTINUUM OF LEARNING:
KEY: C - is consistently achieving objectives
E - is progressing toward objectives as expected
P - needs more practice and experience to meet objectives

☐ Not evaluated at this time

Promoted to: _____

(The interrelated areas of listening, speaking, reading, and writing build upon and support one another.)

	I	II	III
LANGUAGE ARTS			
LISTENING/SPEAKING			
expresses ideas orally with clarity			
listens and comments appropriately			
READING			
chooses to read independently			
understands what is read (summarizes, retells, discusses)			
uses a variety of strategies:			
uses picture clues			
rereads when meaning is unclear			
makes meaningful substitutions			
uses the context			
uses word parts (word families and vowel patterns-phonics)			
self-corrects			
recognizes common words			
reads fluently with expression			
responds to text (orally, in writing, and through the arts)			
uses text to find/state facts, and support opinions			
uses reference materials and resources			
WRITING			
chooses to write regularly			
attempts different kinds of writing (poetry, letters, stories, reflections, etc.)			
enriches own writing using models from literature, adults, and peers			
begins to revise for clarity, focus and organization			
uses details and interesting words			
begins to develop a personal style (voice)			
begins to proofread and edit for capitalization, punctuation, sentence structure, and grammar			
uses spelling strategies to move toward conventional spelling			
spells common words correctly			
writes legibly			

EDUCATIONAL REPORT

	I	II	III
SOCIAL STUDIES			
participates in discussions and activities			
gaining knowledge about the world and people			
understands the four directions and can apply to maps and globes			
creates simple maps with map keys			
gathers and evaluates information from field trips			
understands the geographic relationships between continent, country, state, and city			
identifies and organizes events to their place in the past			
SCIENCE			
obtains information through accurate observation			
groups objects by their similarities and /or differences			
uses information to make valid predictions			
constructs and uses written reports, drawings, diagrams, graphs, or charts to gain information			
HEALTH			
learns and uses appropriate vocabulary			
understands how body senses help us to communicate			
recognizes the importance and need for good nutrition			
recognizes how good health habits prevents disease			
WORK AND STUDY HABITS			
organizes time, work, and personal belongings			
prepares for class with appropriate materials			
completes daily work assignments			
completes homework assignments			
listens and responds appropriately			
follows oral and written directions			
stays on task			
has pride in good workmanship			
SOCIAL & PERSONAL GROWTH			
demonstrates appropriate peer relationships			
uses polite language			
accepts responsibility and consequences for behavior			
cooperates with adults			
works cooperatively with a group			
follows established rules and routines			
respects property			
demonstrates self-control			

14

Chapter 2

Teachers' Philosophies About Teaching and Kids

What Did I Ask and Why?

What is your philosophy of writing report card comments? That is, what do you hope your comments will accomplish? Who are you trying to reach?

These were the questions I asked of eight teachers. I knew that a teacher's philosophy about teaching and assessment would be reflected in her classroom practice. I felt it was important to establish the teacher's point of reference before asking about her actual methods in the classroom.

What Did Teachers Say?

Comments should be positive, teachers said. If it's necessary to point out a weakness or an area that challenges the student, it's best to do so diplomatically and in the context of the child's strengths.

In addition, comments should:

☞ be specific

☞ be tied to instruction

☞ suggest ways in which a parent can assist the child at home or mention ways the teacher is trying to help the child in school

Many teachers feel that report card narratives are crucial for conveying a philosophy of teaching and for communicating the teacher's respect for the child's gifts.

Now let's hear the teachers speak for themselves.

MIN HONG, a first-grade teacher from Manhattan, New York:

A report card is an important document, and you need to back up what you say with examples. If I make a statement such as "Your child is having difficulty focusing," I substantiate it with student samples or actual documents.

Who am I trying to reach? Family members, parents, and most importantly, the child! The report card comments will help the child set goals or give the child something to strive for.

Every report card should be individual, different from the others. I make it very personal so that even if I didn't write the child's name on the report card, the parents still would know it belonged to their child.

I have two personal guidelines when I write a report card comment:

☞ Be positive. (Example: _____ *is becoming a prolific writer.*)

☞ Mention an area in which the child can grow. (Example: _____ *is working hard on his spelling.*)

PENNY STRUBE, a fourth-grade teacher from Hannibal, Missouri:

The purpose of grade card comments is to build confidence a child will find more success the next time or praise the child for the success of the present. Grade card comments should be positive, uplifting, or words of hope for future success. They are global comments.

I believe that there should be no surprise grades on the card. Parents should be aware of a child's strengths and weaknesses throughout the grading period. The grade card's purpose is to confirm the expected grades and create a sense of pride or encouragement for a better quarter to come. Who am I trying to reach? Both parent and child.

If I'm writing a negative note on a report card, I always make sure that I've already contacted the parent about the issue. This way there are no surprises for that parent!

The comments should be personal (about the child's strength of character) and academic.

SUZANNE HOUGHTON VARNEY, a second-grade teacher from New Orleans, Louisiana:

My aim in writing report cards is to give an overview of a child's progress. I'm writing for parents and hope to communicate as straightforwardly as possible. I believe in using supportive language and giving constructive advice about how to address a child's weaknesses.

I always keep in mind that this child is the center of the parent's world. I think about the effect my comment will have on the parents.

A few years ago, when I taught pre-K, I focused my comments more on social behavior and tried to express an understanding of the child's behavior. When I taught Grade 4, I focused more on academic matters.

JANE FOWLER, a fifth-grade teacher from Diamond Bar, California:

I think of myself as an advocate for kids. I look out for the child's well-being. I see it as my responsibility to recognize a strength in that child in at least one area. I want the child to get satisfaction from something he or she does well.

I can sum up my philosophy with this acronym: S.A.F.E.

S = Sensitivity to the parent or guardian and child.

Before I make a comment on a report card, I'm aware of the person who will be reading it. Some children are in situations where a negative comment will bring severe discipline. If that might be the case, I say something positive on the report card and follow up with a telephone call or conference where I discuss my concerns.

A = Affirm what the child can do.

I find the child's strength and state it in the comment. For example, the child may have shown strength in a certain area or have improved in social skills, in playground behavior, or in fine arts.

F = Focus on the most important concern.

If I have a particular concern, I mention it as the student's academic or social challenge. If possible, I address this early in the year so it can be monitored throughout the school year.

E = Every kid is special!

Every kid is unique, so I look for a strength and end the comment on a positive note. Overall, I find something special about the child and share it with the child's parent or guardian.

I also do research into the child's cumulative record cards and talk to past teachers and to the principal or support staff, who give me information to better understand that child. I find that teaching sometimes requires that I be parent, counselor, and in some cases, a most needed friend to my students.

KATHY SHOLTYS, a second-grade teacher from Ithaca, New York:

I hope that my comments are as objective as possible and that they are personal to each child/parent. Narratives should reveal the child's strengths, interests, and areas in need of additional work. Growth should be compared against the individual child, but parents should be aware of how the child fits into their 'developmental level' of growth.

VALERIE WILLIAMS, a first-grade teacher from St. Albans, New York:

Look Back, Look Ahead

Report cards should reflect where the child has been, what has been learned, and goals for the future. Writing report cards forces me to pinpoint exactly where the child is in the learning process. This is the only way the teacher will be able to help parents understand the child's progress in class.

Back Up Materials

I try to write comments that can be documented with test results, work samples, or anecdotal records. Parents react better to comments that are informative without being judgmental.

FRAN MCNULTY, a third-grade teacher from Bayonne, New Jersey:

Sandwich It In

I follow a sandwich approach with my comments:

positive, negative (if necessary), positive.

Hopefully, the positives outweigh the negatives and a parent/guardian realizes that positive statements are to be brought home and discussed with the student as well as the negative ones.

YVONNE SUI RUNYAN, a former teacher of grades K-6 from Boulder, Colorado:

Use It as a Window on Teaching

To me, assessment and evaluation are ways to measure children, but they're also ways to inform us, as teachers, about our own teaching. After all, when writing report cards, we're really dealing with the whole educational process.

Stress Process Over Skills

I think teachers should fashion their report cards to convey to parents the *process* of learning and the strategies we're teaching, not just the skills the child has learned. Parents need to see the big picture. We need to communicate our whole philosophy of teaching.

For example, if the teacher wants to comment on the child's writing, she might say:

> *While drafting a piece, _____ is able to spell correctly any word he wants to use. He's also able to help other students proofread and edit their pieces for spelling. He's looked at by his classmates as an expert in spelling.*
>
> *The part of the process he needs help with is exploring topics of interest and figuring out what it is he wants to say about a particular topic. This approach focuses on the whole process, not just on isolated skills.*

Now that we see the fundamental principles that guide teachers, let's look at the methods they use to actually assess their students' growth.

Chapter 3

Methods for Assessing Our Students

What Did I Ask and Why?

What systems do you or your colleagues use to collect information for report cards?

I knew that the answer to this question would uncover sound systems for collecting information about students and for reporting evaluations fairly to parents.

What Did Teachers Say?

Teachers use a wide range of methods to assess student progress. For example, they rely on portfolios, checklists and inventories, anecdotal records, journals, observations, student self-assessments, and tests.

PENNY STRUBE, Grade 4:

Authentic Evaluation

These are the main ways in which I collect information about my students: I keep anecdotal notes, recorded readings, portfolios, and checklists for each child, and I refer to all of these when I'm writing report card comments.

I keep:

1. **Anecdotal notes** in every subject area, from reading to personal

developments. Examples:

Reading

_____ *seems to be having difficulty focusing on her book during SSR (Sustained Silent Reading). Problem attending to print.*

Math

After one-on-one lesson, _____ has a better understanding of long division.

> *or*

Considerable improvement on long division. Working toward total grasp of long division.

Literature

_____ *shared real insight into the thoughts of the main character. Compared the two main characters.*

> *or*

_____ *discovered the connection between the sequence of events. Made generalizations and synthesized the information. Comprehending at a very high level.*

Social

_____ *misbehaved on the playground. Disagreement with another student. Apologized and regretted incident. Showing real growth.*

Sometimes I record **anecdotal quotes,** too, along with my notes. For example:

_____ *said about Moby Dick: "I liked the ending. It seemed just. Ahab got his Moby, and Moby got his Ahab."*

> *or*

_____ *said: "I get this now. It took me three times, and now I really understand." _____ is experiencing real success in math. This is her weakest subject.*

> *or*

_____ *said: "The boy's stompin' was saying 'I'm hungry.'" _____ did not correct this miscue (stompin' for stomach). He continued to read as though nothing was wrong.*

2. **Recorded readings:** I tape the kids as they read aloud, then I do a miscue analysis.

3. **Portfolios:** Each week children put items in the portfolio so I can analyze growth over time. I use two types of portfolios: growth and showcase.

Growth Portfolio

Early in the school year I start a growth portfolio for each child. I place various items in the portfolio, then collect new items at the intervals shown here:

Items Collected	How Often
creative writing sample	2 per month
handwriting sample	1 per month
reading inventory	first week of school
math inventory	first week of school
literature log (also called journal)	1 per month
research notes to show the child's note-taking process	1 per month
oral reading sample (recorded on cassette)	at end of each piece of literature
interest inventory	first week of school

I collect samples of students' strengths *and* weaknesses. The portfolios are cumulative. At the end of the year, they're very thick.

Showcase Portfolio:

The children are in charge of this portfolio. It contains the best work produced by the child. My students self-evaluate pieces in each of the following disciplines:

theme study: reports, fliers, maps, illustrations, diagrams, other.

math: a piece that shows success in math on at least one concept; a piece the child is proud of keeping.

spelling: a particular set of words that the child spelled on a test.

writing: the most creative piece of writing in fiction, nonfiction, and narrative.

literature log entry: shows their most reflective entry written about a piece of literature.

reading book list: a record kept by children of all the books they read, including title, author, genre, and number of pages.

art: any artwork prized by the student.

4. Checklists: I use checklists as a way to keep track of my students' abilities and weaknesses. I keep two kinds: individual and group.

Sample Individual Checklist: Oral and Written Response to Literature

Name: Thomas

Book: My Side of the Mountain

	4/3	4/5	4/7	4/11	4/13	4/17	4/19	4/21		
KNOWLEDGE										
Setting	X									
Characters	X						X			
Narrator										
Details					X					
COMPREHENSION										
Summarizes	X	X		X						
Sequence		X								
Mood							X			
Main Idea				X						
Figurative Language					X	X				
APPLICATION										
Draws Conclusions				X				X		
Illustrates				X	X					
States Examples								X		
Relates Personally			X	X		X	X	X		
Research										
ANALYSIS										
Compare					X		X	X		
Contrast					X		X	X		
Debate								X		
Makes Generalizations						X		X		
Analyzes Problems										
Cause and Effect						X				
SYNTHESIS										
Constructs New Meaning						X				
Predicts Outcome							X			
Formulates a Solution										
Creates New Ideas										
Writes (story, poem, etc.)										
EVALUATION										
Author's Purpose										
Critique										
Judges w/reasons										
Evaluates w/reasons										
Personal Opinion										

Session Comments:

Individual

Here is an example of an individual checklist. It allows me to observe my students' use of story elements during the reading of a piece of literature. I make a copy of the sheet for each student, write the child's name, then place an X and the date to indicate when the child showed she understood that element. When do I observe students? During our literature discussions and in conversations with the child as she interprets her thoughts in the literature log.

Sometimes I record special comments in the space at the bottom of the sheet.

Sample Group Checklist

Title/Author: *"Tuck Everlasting" by Natalie Babbit*

Student Names	Comes prepared for group	Has read assignment	Has written in Lit. Log	Shares thoughts and ideas		
Natalie	X	X	X	X		
Robyn	X	X	X	X		
Jesse	X	X	X	X		
Jennifer	X	X		X		
Valerie		X	X			
Nathan		X		X		

Observable Items

Sample "Yes/No" Checklist

Name: *Levi*　　　　　　　　　　　Date: *April 21*

	Yes	No
Reads by choice	X	
Is prepared for lit. group	X	
Discusses with group	X	
Shares personal opinion		X

Group

I also use group checklists (*left*).

In addition to gridlike checklists, I sometimes use a Yes/No sheet of observable behaviors (*below*) or multiple options checklists (*page 26*):

Sample Multiple Options Checklist

Name: *Levi*

Book: *"Tuck Everlasting"*

	Never	Seldom	Sometimes	Usually	Always
Analyzes characters			X		
Makes predictions			X		
Connects situations				X	
Constructs new meaning			X		
Shares personal opinion		X			
Illustrates setting					X
Identifies cause and effect			X		
Compares/contrasts				X	
Reveals the author's purpose	X				
Debates issues		X			

VALERIE WILLIAMS, Grade 1:

I gather information through:

Test results: For example, end-of-book tests in reading or unit tests in math.

Journals: I examine children's math journals and daily writing journals.

Anecdotal records: I keep a folder for each child. I make notes on self-stick notes and place them in folders at the end of the week.

MIN HONG, Grade 1:

I assess my students in formal and informal ways throughout the year. I look to see which children have grasped a concept and which children need help. I may even look for an alternate way to teach a concept to meet the learning style of a particular child. All of these contribute to my picture of the child. I'll mention some of these on the report card.

Some of the methods I use include portfolios, anecdotal notes, and conferences. Let me explain.

1. Portfolios

When I'm writing the report card, I look through the child's portfolio for evidence of growth.

Every other month I place in the child's folder samples of his or her work. Some items in the portfolio are selected by the child; others are selected by me. This is the system I use:

Child's Selection

In November, March, and June I meet with each child to help them choose one piece of writing to add to the writing section of the portfolio. I ask the child to choose a piece that *shows their growth as a writer.*

I also ask the child to select a piece that *shows their best work*, along with a statement of "Why I Like It." Children include statements like "I like it because it's funny" or "I like it because it's about my cat." This shows me what kind of learner the child is.

Teacher's Selection

Periodically I look through each child's work on my own to assess their growth and spot areas of need. I choose writing pieces that show all areas—including spelling, topic selection, mechanics, and so forth. Of course, when I see an area in which the child needs help, such as leaving too little space between words, I give that child extra attention. I may or may not mention this on the report card, but it's an option that's available to me.

2. Observation

I make brief notes about children's work, which I take as I circulate around the room during writing time, during Daily News time, or in informal conversations with them. In addition, I look at the child's writing in the content areas—for example, science and social studies—and make notes.

3. Conferences

When a child has written a story and feels he is ready to edit it, we meet for a five- to fifteen-minute editing conference. The child reads his work to me and we talk about areas he feels he needs help with (examples: matching the title with the story, use of punctuation or plurals). I take notes as we confer and use them to record growth over a period of time.

10/6 Rosie — Writing more fluently now. More enthusiastic about her stories. Reads stories aloud with expression.

10/13 Rosie — Science writing shows confusion about steps in a process. Will have another conference with her to help her number the steps.

1/20 Rosie — During Daily News time, she read story about package from California fluently.

Susan   9/12
Got started right away.
Wrote story re: missing her
best friend. Risk taking
space — needs work.
Got stuck on d _ d. To
continue story, (S) asked
to talk about her thoughts
before writing.

Frank   9/13
Excell risk taking. Wrote a
story about "Walking on a Hot
Day" Experim. w/ letters
(stringing letters/chunks)
Doesn't want to share his
writing w/class. Work on labeling.

Tanya   9/12
Beautiful illus. Very detailed.
Avoids writing with support—
begins to write. Some sight
words (the, and, a) Initi
cons. Use pictures / Illus.
to get her motivated or to
begin taking risks.

Other Areas

Math

I use two pieces of formal assessment, such as tests or checklists. The checklists contain areas such as "counts by 5s" and "understands one-to-one correspondence."

Reading

Besides keeping inventories, I also have my students complete these statements: "I did a good job on _____" and "I need to work on _____." Sometimes I jot down quotes from the child.

Name: _____ Date:_____
In looking at my _____

I did a great job on . . .	I need to work on . . .

Art

I keep selected samples in their portfolio. For instance, a child who loves to draw or paint or make a puppet can put that product in the portfolio. It does not have to be a finished work.

SUZANNE HOUGHTON VARNEY, Grade 2:

In addition to keeping folders for each child, I keep a notebook in which I place anecdotal comments. As I observe my students, I write these comments on mailing label-sized stickers and then place them on the appropriate pages in my notebook.

JANE FOWLER, Grade 5:

Life Folders

I use what I call Life Folders to keep parents informed about the weekly progress of their child. When the report card arrives, there are no surprises.

I create a Life Folder for each child during the first week of school. On one side of the manila folder I place a weekly letter to parents. Written by me, it reminds parents of school events. On the other side I place a check sheet on which the child sets goals for himself or herself. It's labeled "Week of _____." I add comments to the child's goals, and the entire folder goes home.

"Every week the child places in the folder all work that has been graded. The child takes the folder home on Mondays. I ask the parents to review the work and, together with the child, decide if any work should be included in the child's portfolio (which is a separate folder). If the parent likes a piece of work, she places a P in the upper right hand side of the

Dear Parents,

To improve communication between school and home, I have started your child's "Life Folders." Every other Monday a folder will be sent home with our child with his or her work in it for your review. There will not be great quantities of work because a lot of work is done in journals at school.

Please review your child's work and read my comments, if any. Sign and make any comments you wish, and return the folder to school with your child on Tuesday.

Thank you,

Mrs. Fowler.

Name: _____ Week Of:_____

Day	Notes	Whole Language	Social Science	Science	Math	Parent's Initials
M O N						
T U E S						
W E D						
T H U R S						
F R I						

Writing words:: _____ _____ _____

_____ _____

Weekly goals: _____

_____

I'm reading: _____

I'm writing: _____

paper. If the student likes the paper, he places an S, and I make my selection with a T. The child returns the paper to school on Tuesday.

I like to ask parents what they think of the Life Folder. The comments I receive are always positive.

FRAN MCNULTY, Grade 3:

I use anecdotal records, portfolios, and other assessment tools. Let me explain:

Anecdotal Records

On self-stick notes I write comments to myself. After a while I have a lot of information about my students.

Reading Portfolios, General Portfolios, Book Report Portfolios

Every six to eight weeks we do housecleaning. I look at the quality of my student's work. I look for improvement. With all those student samples, the evidence of improvement is right in front of me.

I often write comments to my students while scanning their papers. I encourage my students to write back to me.

Other

To assess children's development, I also use matrix sheets from commercial publishers.

YVONNE SUI RUNYAN, Grades K–6:

I can tell you about my use of anecdotal records, conferences, Status of Class Report, and student self-evaluation:

Anecdotal Records

When I was in the classroom, I used an anecdotal record book in which I recorded information. I was especially interested in areas in which a child was struggling and in the child's AHAs! (new discoveries). These gave me in-depth knowledge about the child's progress which may otherwise have gotten lost. Once a week I made anecdotal notes for each child.

Teacher-Student Conferences

I also had a conference once a week with each student. At that time, I jotted down information in each child's folder.

Status of Class Report

One of the most fruitful systems I used was the Status of Class Report.

This helped me to understand where kids were in different areas. For example, if I was concentrating on writing, I'd ask the class, "How are you planning to spend workshop time today?" If a child often said "I'm going to work on getting a good lead," I'd know this was an area that was important to him. In fact, the children's answers to that question also indicated to me how I should spend my time teaching. If many students said they were spending time on dialogue or on leads, then I recognized a pattern and knew I needed to teach more mini-lessons on the subject.

Roger

11/4 Roger noticing character development in Scott O'Dell's Island of the Blue Dolphins. He continues to follow me around the room, reading aloud an especially poignant moment in the book. When the character says or does something strong, Roger says to me, "Listen to this!" Then he reads the excerpt out loud.

11/6 During writing workshop, Roger said to me, "I want to learn how authors develop their characters. Can you help me do that?" I said I couldn't help him, but asked "Who could you go to for help? Roger understood that he should study the author's techniques.

11/13 Roger wrote a new story today in writing workshop. Story shows stronger character development. Roger understands how to learn from authors.

Student Self-Evaluation

For each quarterly report, I'd ask kids in Grades 1–6 to write goals for each subject area—that is, to self-evaluate. I'd attach that to the report card. I asked the children to go into their portfolios and reflect on three things:

☞ what they did well

☞ what they needed to improve on

☞ their goals

Other

I also used learning logs, tests, long-term projects, student portfolios, writing samples, and miscue analysis.

Summary

I've always felt that it's important to communicate to parents my philosophy of teaching, the *process* of education, not just skills taught. So if a child often said to me "I'm having trouble finding a good topic for writing," I may have written on the report card: _____ *needs help in rehearsing good topics.*

I used what I learned about the child through conversations, conferences, work samples, and the Status of Class Report to write comments.

Chapter 4

Tips for Writing Report Card Narratives

What Did I Ask and Why?

What suggestions would you offer to other teachers about writing report card comments? Can you give examples?

I was certain that the answers to these questions would elicit specific examples of exemplary report card comments and would include a rationale as to why these comments are effective.

How Did Teachers Respond?

"Offer praise and encouragement for the child's efforts," teachers said, "and call attention to the child's strengths." Teachers agreed that it's important to point out the positive ways in which that child is unique. Let's hear this in the teachers' own words.

PENNY STRUBE, Grade 4:

Provide Encouragement

I try to be as positive as possible. Even if there's a negative I have to mention, I always give the child "reasons for hope." I might say, *Your child is working hard on showing growth in _____.*

I try to give the child as much encouragement as I can. For example, if I've written a negative comment, I may also attach a cute Garfield™ sticker to the report card, on which I write: *I know you worked hard, even though you still haven't grasped those science concepts.* I do that so as to recognize the child's efforts. This gives the child a pick-me-up.

Assess the Student, Praise the Child

I always address two areas—academic and social. I write positive statements like:

_____ *has grown in her understanding of math concepts. She works hard and I appreciate that she stays after school for extra help.*

and

_____ *is delightful in class. She's energetic, helpful, and a community builder.*

Include Helpful Strategies

If there's a major problem for the child, I find that the space for the comments on the report card is too small. So I attach to the report card a sheet of strategies that the parents can use to teach the child at home. The note may say:

Next quarter we're starting over. Here are some reading strategies that will help your child read better. When your child gets home from school each day, perhaps you can work with her on these areas.

KATHY SHOLTYS, Grade 2:

Be Objective

I make my comments objective and personal for each child. Examples:

For Work Habits:

_____ *has found a balance between work time and playtime. He takes responsibility for solving his work-related questions.*

or

_____ *is able to finish a task with a clearly defined beginning and ending. It is difficult for her to successfully finish an assignment that is open-ended.*

For Math:

_____ *is able to tell time to the hour and half hour. I am working with him to tell time to the quarter hour.*

Attach Work Samples

In addition to the comments themselves, I often include a work sample by the child or a written description of what he or she does well or finds challenging.

MIN HONG, Grade 1:

Avoid Jargon

Be thoughtful of the language you use with parents. Use simple, common language, not teacher jargon. For example, I would never use technical terms because parents may not know what they mean. That kind of language would cause a divide between teachers and parents. Words and phrases I wouldn't use: *writing process, decoding, one-to-one correspondence,* and *book talk* (unless I had sent home notes about what a book talk is.)

VALERIE WILLIAMS, Grade 1:

Be Specific

A report card should note observable behavior, not just general impressions. So if you say:

_____ *is making great strides in reading*

back it up with details such as:

_____ *stays on task and is able to use a variety of reading strategies. He's particularly good at using context clues.*

_____ *is able to apply prior knowledge to new topics.*

_____ *reads with fluid expression.*

JANE FOWLER, Grade 2:

Involve Parents

I always bring parents "in" on my report card comments. I make parents a part of the educational process. One way I do that is by inviting parents to write comments on their child's weekly Life Folders. (For information on Life Folders, see Chapter 3.) Another way is by thanking parents—directly or indirectly— on the report card itself. I may say it simply:

Thanks for all your help this year.

Treat With Respect

I look at each child as distinct, not as a "fill-in-the-blank." When I write a report card comment, I think, "If this were *my* child, how would I want him or her to be treated?"

SUZANNE HOUGHTON VARNEY, Grade 2:

Convey Child's Specialness

Always convey something unique about the child. Show what you appreciate about that boy or girl, such as his integrity or her personality. Show that you're excited about the child's progress and invested in the child's development.

Examples:

_____ *is growing in self-confidence.*
I'm really excited to see this happen.

_____ *has made good progress in social studies this year.*

It has been exciting to observe _____*'s growth as a reader over the past few months.*

> "*Always convey something unique about the child.*"

Enlist Parents' Help

If you mention a child's weakness, end with a suggestion as to how the family can address the problem. That is, try to put a positive spin on things.

Example: If you write: _____ *has trouble focusing on his homework,* you can add: *Perhaps you can help him find a quieter spot in his room to filter out distractions.*

Use Lots of Details

Cite specific examples of a child's work and progress, such as:

During Writing Workshop, _____ *goes right to the task of putting her ideas down on paper. She has particularly enjoyed experimenting with poetry. She applies to her poems what we have learned about similes, metaphors, and repetition.*

_____ *uses mental strategies to solve addition and subtraction problems.*

_____ *has a strong grasp of the science concepts we have covered this term.*

_____ *finds it difficult at times to focus. It's helpful to have him sit near the front of the room.*

_____ *is a great contributor to our reading and history discussions. His ability to recall and apply previously discussed ideas shows how carefully he listens and absorbs the new material on our state's history.*

In math, _____ *shows a firm grasp of basic operations and the money and place value concepts we are reviewing. She is able to cover a good deal of material, often going beyond the minimum to help run the cash register in our class store.*

Use Common Sense
Avoid critical words, like *ill-behaved, annoying,* and *noisy.*

VALERIE WILLIAMS, Grade 1:

Record Observable Behavior
For example:

_____ *is able to remember and follow directions necessary for completion of independent assignments.*

_____ *is a very talented student who is confident enough in her skills to experiment and take risks. When given a more open-ended task, such as a project or writing assignment, she adds her original ideas. The results are as imaginative, such as a humorous drawing of a turkey with chicken pox.*

Highlight a Unique Aspect of Each Child
For example:

_____ *frequently acts as a leader during free activity periods.*

_____ *particularly enjoys our discussions of books. He loved our read-aloud book* Owen, *and read it on his own as well.*

YVONNE SIU RUNYAN, Grades K–6:

Start With Something Positive
I like to begin with something about the child's personality or characteristics, then move to the academic areas.
Examples:

_____ *makes friends easily. Her peers look to her for advice, assurance,* and even direction. She is doing especially well in music and language arts. The areas that challenge her are science and social studies. While she is able to understand the reading materials, _____ has a difficult time drawing conclusions about what she has read.

Use Concrete Examples

_____ uses a "circle" plot structure for all of her stories. I am working with her to use other organizational structures in her writing. I'm helping her use a beginning, a middle, and an end in some stories.

Chapter 5

Words and Phrases That Work

What Did I Ask and Why?

What phrases or words do you often use when writing comments? Why are these effective?

It was clear that teachers value positive comments. Perhaps they would suggest useful sentence starters that reflect that. I also looked for other words and phrases that would offer a fresh approach to report card writing.

What Did Teachers Say?

Above all, choose words that encourage children. On the following pages is a combined list of words and phrases that teachers find effective, grouped by message. Some words are appropriate for more than one category.

> Words that encourage kids and parents— and that are positive—include: *energetic, consistent, hard worker, problem-solver, risk-taker, potential, engaging, persevering, creative*

41

Keep It Positive!

thorough	has a good grasp of
caring	independent learner
truthful	works hard
cooperative	improved tremendously
shows expertise in	striving
is able to	seeking
shows commitment	attempting
is willing to take more risks	admirable
growth	genuine
superior	does a great job with
quality	excels at
is strong in	making good progress

Examples:

_____ *is making good progress with his alphabetizing skills. He knows how to alphabetize to the second letter and is beginning to use a dictionary to locate word meanings.*

_____ *relies less on the teacher for the spelling of unknown words.*

_____'s *work reflects careful attention to detail and presentation.*

Appreciate Child's Unique Qualities

interacts well with peers	imaginative
problem-solver	shows compassion
interested in	sets a standard for others
positive attitude	persistent
thinks clearly	diplomatic
understands complex tasks	innovative
risk-taker	cooperative
creative	selects carefully

original

concentrates well

generates many original ideas

follows directions carefully

suggests new approaches

leader

thoughtful

enthusiastic

perceptive

eager

fluent reader

intrigued by

welcomes

special talent for

is skilled in

follows projects through to

Example:

_____'s ideas for stories are so original. He thinks his ideas through and makes careful selections before he begins. He also has a good sense of story structure and knows how to include exciting elements in the plot, which draws his readers in.

Child Needs Extra Help

could profit by

requires

finds it difficult at times to

it is helpful to

needs reinforcement in

shows a need for

thrives on

is challenged by

works best when

needs help with

I'm working with him (her) to

benefits from

responds well to

has difficulty with

encourage her (him) to

has trouble with

making progress

Let's find a way to solve this together.

I'm enclosing his (her) weekly report.

Examples:

_____ continues to show growth in his writing. We will continue to help him add details to his creative writing stories.

_____ shows more self-confidence and is more willing to confront problems directly on his own.

This is useful for a child with a behavior problem:

> *_____ has worked hard to improve his behavior in class. When he really tries, he can stay on task. He benefits from the individual attention you give him at night.*

Verbs That Convey Child's Actions

does/did	recognizes	relates
can	uses	solves
remembers	selects	identifies
associates	gives	compares
applies	locates	contrasts
expresses	creates	appreciates

Phrases That Build Bridges to Families

Thanks for your help.

I appreciate your _____.

I'm trying to help her by _____.

I have been excited to see your child's growth in _____.

Feel free to make an appointment to see me.

I look forward to our conference next Wednesday at __ a.m./p.m.

Examples:

> *_____'s oral reading has improved this quarter. Thank you for practicing with him daily at home.*

> *Your continued support of _____ at home has helped him reach his weekly goals.*

> *_____'s facility with math facts has improved now that you are giving her an extra five minutes of practice every night.*

> *Thanks for letting me know about _____'s special interest in frogs. I have a number of good books on that subject and will try to encourage him to read them.*

44

Your weekend cooking sessions with _____ have helped her reading. _____ chooses cookbooks from the school library and enjoys reading them during DEAR (Drop Everything and Read) time in class.

Words to Be Wary Of

unable	won't	never
can't	always	

Words to Use Instead

has difficulty with	seldom
seems reticent about	usually
needs encouragement in	has a tendency to

Adam Berkin, a former fourth-grade teacher in Brooklyn, New York, shares a list of comments that he has compiled over the years. He says that referring to the list has made writing report cards easier—and less time-consuming.

Writing

informative pieces are well developed

displays research skills

incorporates models from literature

uses notes and plans to assist in expression of ideas

uses complex sentence forms and starts to set out writing in paragraphs

starts to build plot, suspense, characters, dialogue, setting, purpose, and climax into narrative

willingly takes suggestions from peers and teacher

learning to take meaningful notes

makes use of descriptive language

is developing correct capitalization, punctuation, and sentence structure

has begun to edit for mechanics

benefits from feedback and questions and revises effectively

self edits

writes legibly

uses invented spelling in early drafts but searches for correct form before presentation

can write with imaginative touches

willingly shares writing

is developing own voice

sees writing as a tool for learning

takes risks

able to give constructive feedback to a classmate's draft

Reading

usually chooses books with simple narrative

often rereads favorite books

needs help with using reference and information books

is a confident reader who feels at home with books

can use information in books for reference purposes but needs help with unfamiliar material

capable of reading some demanding texts

reads thoughtfully and appreciates shades of meaning

is an enthusiastic and reflective reader who has strong established tastes

enjoys pursuing own reading interests independently

can handle a wide range and variety of texts

contributes thoughtful comments to literature discussions

is respectful of others' comments and builds on them well

can get lost in a book

chooses to read during free time

shares reading experiences with classmates

can articulate why enjoys story

makes reasonable predictions

turns to text to verify and clarify ideas

can talk meaningfully about characters, setting, mood, incident, structure, symbol, time, tensions

makes connections with other books

reads with expression

Discussion

listens attentively and responds to peer comments in discussions

actively participates in group

sensitive to the group members' ideas and views

willing to compromise if necessary to best accomplish a goal

helps others to understand assignments

Work Habits

is productive and involved during work times

expresses enjoyment as a result of hard work and achievement

sensitive to and respectful of others

Chapter 6

What Do Parents Want?

"The vast majority of families care deeply about their children's education and want them to do well in school. Generally, families want to know how their children are "doing" in the basic subjects, especially reading, language arts (including spelling), and mathematics. They want to know if their children are applying themselves, if they are 'behaving' well, and if they are getting along well with others."

—Glennie Buckley, *Report Card on Report Cards*

What Did I Ask Parents?

The parents I spoke with were eager to talk, needing few questions to prompt them to "open up."
Of each parent I asked:

☞ What do you expect when you read your child's report card?

☞ Do you have any overall suggestions for improving report card comments?

☞ What would you like teachers in general to know about your reaction to report card comments?

What Did Parents Say?

Overall, parents approached our talks globally, focusing on the teacher's reporting process in general rather than on the report card in particular. In addition to mentioning report cards, parents made reference to parent-teacher conferences, notes, calls home, and their overall impression of their child's education. When I felt the conversation drifting to general areas, I steered it back to the report card.

Let's hear the parents' own words.

Parent of sixth-grade boy and third-grade girl:

I keep my children's report cards in large boxes, along with special mementos from babyhood on up. I've got their baby photos, preschool projects, school photos, awards, special projects, and stories they've written. From time to time we take them out and look at everything.

Overall, I've been happy with my children's report cards. But if there's a problem, I expect the teacher will let me know as soon as she knows. I wouldn't want to be informed of a problem in the third marking period that started in the first marking period. I expect the teacher will drop me a note or phone me right away to talk about it.

To tell you the truth, some of my friends—who have kids in my kids' classes—expect the teacher to write something "profound" on the report card. I really don't. After all, they've got an awful lot of students. On the other hand, I also feel disappointed if I read something very general, like "Have a nice summer."

. . . Last year the principal made a brief comment on my son's and my daughter's report cards. I was impressed! It made our whole family feel special. After all, with all those kids in the school, the principal took the time to do that.

Mother of two daughters, one in 4th grade, the other in 6th grade:

For several years my daughter came home from school with wonderful report cards. I call them the $10,000 report cards because they were so outstanding. I felt like showing the report to everyone I knew.

The problem was that they didn't zero in on any one area. I'd read a one- or two-line statement from the main teacher and from the art, dance, and gym teachers, respectively. But they were general and not all that helpful. What's more, the dance teacher wrote for every kid, "Your child adds a lot to dance class." I expected a more specific, individualized comment for my child.

In the last few years the report card comments have gotten more specific, and I appreciate that. Now I know *exactly* where my child is in each subject.

. . . One year, a teacher mentioned on the report card a low score

(65%) my daughter received on a standardized test. I was upset that the teacher wrote that, as I saw it as a stigma that the score would forever be "in print."

Mother of two grown sons:

Both my sons went to a traditional private school. The emphasis there was on becoming literate, and the school did a good job with teaching reading, writing, and math. My boys did well academically.

But I wish the report card had raised questions about another aspect of my sons' development: self-confidence. Today one of my sons has a serious problem with that. I wonder if the school knew the early warning signals. If so, I wish they had brought it to my attention. I wouldn't have wanted them to scare me, but I wish they'd have focused equally hard on his social development. I wish the school had raised questions about this, then presented me with some options for how to handle it. After all, they're the professionals.

Oddly enough, my (problem) son excelled in school and did as he was told. But those kind of kids are often the ones who need special attention. The teachers emphasized social development in the early grades, but that aspect took a back seat as the kids went up the grades.

Today that son is a first-semester freshman at a prestigious college. But I hold out little hope that he will stay in college for more than one term. He has a major problem with drugs—he has for years—and it's tearing my family apart.

Parent of two grown children who is an educational consultant:

As a parent and a teacher, my experiences with my two children in school were quite different. With my daughter, the report card was like a badge of honor: it showed, in written form, that my daughter was at the top of her class.

But with my son, the report card was often a shock. The comments described a boy I did not know. The report card said my son "talks out of turn in class," "does not stay on task," and that "he's a wise guy." But at home I had a son who was inquisitive, verbal, and interested in all sorts of things. When I went to school to talk about these issues with his teacher, I changed from being an articulate adult to feeling like a third grader myself. When I left those meetings, I never knew whether to blame my son or myself. I felt I was being told I was not a good parent . . . I was scared. I didn't have the answers but I'm proud of my children today.

. . . As a middle-class parent and teacher, I wish the teacher had asked me what works well for me at home. I wish the teacher had asked me for advice. Thinking back, that teacher would have gotten further with me if she had said, "What are you doing successfully at home with your son that I can emulate in my classroom?" This would have been positive and emphasized that I was doing a good job all along. . .

. . . Nowadays, portfolios are a big addition to parent-teacher conferences. Today we teachers use the old reporting systems, but we back them up with student portfolios. It's a step in the right direction.

What Do Parents Look for in Report Card Comments? What Can You Do to Address That?

☞ How is my child special?

Teacher's action: Make the report card for each child unique. Offer specific comments about each child. Avoid general comments that also appear on other children's report cards.

☞ How can I help my child improve academically and socially?

Teacher's action: Offer concrete suggestions. Distribute a lists of books parents can read aloud to their child at home. Suggest short activities (read the paper together after dinner), as well as long-range activities (visit the library or enroll the child in a sports program).

☞ Is my child doing okay?

Teacher's action: Communicate often with families. If a child is having difficulty, let the parent know as early in the school year as possible. They want to be able to tackle a problem early on and parents feel frustrated if they find out a problem may have existed for months prior to issuing the report card.

Chapter 7

Strategies for Resolving Possible Problems

Most teachers, at some point in their careers, will send home a report card that stirs up a parent's concern—even anger. (What do you mean my child is failing in math—she's a genius! How can you say my child instigates fights with classmates? He never does that at home!) All the teachers I spoke with said that the report card is not the forum to *first* inform parents of a child's struggles. But, they advised, when you have to put a child's academic or social weaknesses on record, it's what you communicate to parents *before* and *after* the report card that counts. Here, additional teachers share their strategies for communicating with parents of children who are going through a rocky time.

Child Struggling Academically

Start-of-Year Conferences

PEGGY SCOTT, a second-grade teacher in Brookline, Massachusetts:

I start the year by establishing a relationship with parents and use that as a basis for all future interactions. When, or if, I have special issues to discuss with parents, they already know that I like and respect their child. After Labor Day, and during the first week of school, I send a letter to parents inviting them to a conference (held in the morning, before the kids have arrived for the day). The meeting is voluntary. I ask parents to talk to me about what they feel worked and didn't work for their child the year before. That way, we start off with a reference point for the relationship we'll have throughout the coming year.

As the year progresses, I let parents know what the child does well and where the child is experiencing difficulty. If the child isn't progressing well, I'll be specific on the report card but I won't overwhelm the parent.

Suggest Home Activities

I sometimes suggest a way a parent can help at home (because sometimes parents don't realize just how helpful they can be). For example, if a child is having trouble generalizing, or if he's limited by his own experiences, I'll suggest that the parent read to that child a book that broadens his experiences (such as a book on different kinds of homes). Or I'll tell the parent about a topic we're studying in class and ask the parent to talk to the child about how that's connected to the child's life at home.

Suggest One Strategy, Then Follow Up

I suggest one home strategy, then follow up in a month or so to see if the child responds well. For example, if I have suggested that the parent ask the child one reading question every night, I'll also suggest that the parent check back with me in four weeks so we can see how this is working.

Focus on One Issue at a Time

The most important thing is to be honest and not give misinformation. But I wouldn't say to a parent "*Everything* is terrible. Your child is sinking." In fact, at different times during the year I might talk about different things that aren't going well.

MARY GALLIVAN, a former fourth-grade teacher in New York City:

In Addition to Report Cards, Use Portfolios to Communicate With Parents

Portfolios are a way of demonstrating to parents the child's strengths and areas in need of improvement. The teachers in my school who are most effective have their students address strengths *and* weaknesses in the portfolios so the kids themselves are also involved in assessing their progress.

We start the self-reflection process at the beginning of the year. I have students write a Weekly Reflection, which addresses what children think they did well on and areas they wanted to work on. Then, during the parent-teacher conference, the parents and I discuss these and looked at the documents as well.

Child Displays Social Problems

PEGGY SCOTT, Grade 2:

Be Neutral but Accurate

If a child is acting out in class, I might say on the report card, *Your child is not available for instruction. It's hard to give a fair and clear indication of how your child is doing academically. For example, your child isn't able to follow directions because she seems to be distracted by _____. Here's what I'd recommend . . . .*

Involve Guidance Counselor

If I feel a child's problems go beyond my realm, I'll go to the guidance counselor for a referral or a diagnosis. The guidance counselor may suggest that the parent take the child to a pediatrician or to a mental health professional for short-term counseling. But the guidance counselor and I would make sure the timing is right for this.

Keep Teacher Journal

I keep a journal in which I record anecdotes about the child's behavior. That way I can refer to it when I'm writing report cards or talking with a parent.

GLORIA HOYOS, a Title 1 coordinator teacher in El Paso, Texas:

Make Use of Teacher Observation Form

A teacher has to be careful when making comments on the report card. After all, comments may follow a child for a long time. For example, if a child moves from one school to another, or to another district, the parent is often asked to bring with her the child's report card. That's used as a basis for the child's placement in the new school.

A teacher should always write comments that reflect consistent behavior. The teacher shouldn't write something that happened just a few days before the teacher filled out the card. One way to safeguard against this is to periodically fill in a teacher observation form (noting the dates) and back that up with examples of the child's work. For example, if you write that the child "is having difficulty focusing," you should be able to substantiate that in several ways.

Keep in mind that children often change from one year to another. If the parents of a child in grade 4 are going through a divorce, the child may exhibit social or academic problems in class. But the next year, in grade 5, the mother may have remarried a real nice guy, and the child may not display those problems anymore.

ADAM BERKIN, Grade 4:

It's All in the Phrasing

If you have a student who is a real bully, it's tempting to call a spade a spade, but of course, you can't. You do have to be honest with parents, though, especially if the child's behavior is disrupting the class. If I have a student who is often mean toward others, I'll write, "is not always sensitive to others' feelings." If I notice a child gossips, I might say, "has difficulty forming trust in friendships" or "repeats things that can be hurtful to others." If a child fools around a lot, I'd say, "is easily distracted by others."

Adversarial Parent

PEGGY SCOTT, Grade 2:

Be Professional

Sometimes a parent may accuse the teacher of not helping the child satisfactorily and come to school to tell her that the child's poor report card is actually the fault of the teacher. In a case like that, it's important for us to be the professionals, to show graciousness, and to step back a bit. In fact, all the skills you have for being a good listener would come into effect during such a meeting. Remember, the parent feels even more vulnerable than we do. After all, this is his or her child.

During the conference, I would acknowledge what the parent feels but stand my ground as well. I'd say, "I hear what you're saying, but I see your child differently from 8 A.M. to 2 P.M. in school. I'm basing my assessment on my observations of your child and what I know about children. But this is a good time to put our heads together and find a solution." Then the parent and I would try to find a way to help that boy or girl.

Parent Puts Pressure on Child

MARY GALLIVAN:

Involve the Principal

The students in my class were always so on top of things, yet the parents often wanted them to work harder still. The parents sometimes put so much pressure on the kids to do better on their report cards and elsewhere that the expectations for the kids were enormous. (Sometimes the parents didn't mind what was written on the report card. They were more concerned with how the child did on the city-wide tests.)

To deal with that, I had running dialogues with the principal of my school, informing her of what I considered undue pressures on kids. As a result, the principal, who was quite supportive, would walk by my room in the mornings and chat with parents, letting them know that their expectations were, in our opinion, damaging to their children, and asking that they ease up. In some cases, this helped.

Child Disorganized

LESLIE STERLING:

Show and Tell

Sometimes I'll have a child who is quite disorganized—everything is falling out of her desk, she forgets to bring lunch, things are flying all over the place, she doesn't bring in the right assignments, or she doesn't write down the homework assignment. In a case like that, I'll write on the report card that "_____ needs to work on organizational skills that affect her work in all curriculum areas." But I'll also bring the parent in and show her the child's desk. That usually speaks volumes. In many cases, the parent isn't all that shocked at the news. She'll say, "This doesn't surprise me. You should see her room at home!"

Chapter 8

Guidelines, Formats, Schedules, and Tips

Here are some basic recommendations for writing effective comments. Many teachers find this structure helpful.

Suggested Format

a. Start with something positive. Comment on the child's academic and/or social progress.

b. Describe in observable terms the child's strengths, improvements, growth, or successes, giving reasons to celebrate and encourage the child to make further strides.

c. If necessary, cite in specific terms an area that challenges the child and tell how you are trying to help.

d. Encourage parental involvement by suggesting how Moms and Dads can help their child, or thank the parents for the help they have already given.

Examples:

_____ *has made impressive growth this term as a reader. Her sight word vocabulary has expanded dramatically, and she reads more now. We are working on using the context of a sentence to figure out unknown words. Thanks for exposing her to a good deal of children's literature at home. _____ uses this background in her book discussions in class.*

It has been exciting to watch _____'s growing enjoyment of writing these past few months. She is proud of her recent story about her trip to Disneyland, in which she used imaginative details about the exhibits, the hotel, and dinner out. I am working with her to apply writing conventions (such as punctuation and capitalization) as she edits her work. Perhaps you can help at home by reviewing words that need capital letters and by pointing out the use of periods and commas.

_____ very much enjoyed our science unit on leaves. He especially liked comparing leaf samples from the school yard with those in his backyard and found it easy to classify samples by color, size, shape, edge, and veins. I am working with him on handling materials in the science center without hurting others. Perhaps you can discuss with him safe ways to use these tools.

Write a Few Per Week

If you're like me, you prepare for report card writing by going through the assessment materials you have collected for each child. Then you sit down and craft comments carefully, basing them on your complete picture of that boy or girl.

This is a task that takes a good deal of time and energy. In order to give the job the attention it deserves, you can create a schedule in which you write only a few cards per week.

Keep in Mind

Make sure your comments about academic progress are tied to instruction.

Example:

_____'s reading comprehension has improved over the last few months. When seeing a new word, _____ tries to figure it out by looking at it in context. I am trying to encourage her to read more carefully

Sample Writing Schedule

Weeks Before Report Cards Are Distributed:	Write:
5	5 cards
4	5 cards
3	5 cards
2	5 cards
1	5 cards
that week	5 cards
Total	30 cards

By avoiding the writing of 30 (or so) report cards in a short period of time, you will feel less rushed. When the day arrives to distribute your work, you will be able to hand out report cards that make a real difference in children's lives.

Stagger Distribution

You can even speak to your principal about creating a flexible schedule. Rather than handing out all report cards on the same day, your principal may agree to this:

Week:	Distribute report cards of children with:
1	Last names from A–G
2	Last names from H–N
3	Last names from O–R
4	Last names from S–Z

Invite Principal's Comments

If yours is like my former school, your principal may review the report cards you've written and then write comments of his or her own. This is a fine way for the principal to keep up-to-date on students' progress, and it reinforces good school-community relations. If your principal doesn't yet do so, perhaps you should suggest it. Parents and students really appreciate it!

Supplement With Student Samples

If your students have been keeping portfolios, you may want to send home sample documents with the report card or use portfolio items from class as a basis for parent-teacher or student-led conferences. You may show parents a child's best work thus far, or go over before-and-after samples that indicate how much the child has learned over time.

Consider Everlasting Impact

As you compose your students' report cards, keep in mind, as I do, the words of one dedicated teacher and former student:

"A child may keep her report card for a lifetime. In fact, my own mother saved every report card I ever received as a kid. When I look back at my report cards, I always flip mine over and read the comments on the back: what my teachers said about me. To me, report cards are precious documents."

Indeed they are. And *so* much more.

Bibliography

Association of Supervision and Curriculum Development Yearbook. *Communicating Student Progress*. Arlington, VA: ASCD, 1996.

Buckley, Glennie. "First Steps: Redesigning Elementary Report Cards" in Azwell, Tara and Elizabeth Schmar, editors. *Report Card on Report Cards: Alternatives to Consider*. Portsmouth, NH: Heinemann, 1995, pp. 37–48.

Educational Leadership. Vol. 52, no. 2 (October 1994). "Reporting What Students Are Learning."

Guskey, Thomas. "Reporting on Student Learning: Lessons From the Past—Prescriptions for the Future." *ASCD Yearbook* 1996: Communicating Student Learning, pp. 13–24.

Fiderer, Adele. *Practical Assessments for Literature-Based Reading Classrooms*. New York: Scholastic Inc., 1995.

Lake, Kathy and Kafka, Kery. "Reporting Methods in Grades K–8." *ASCD Yearbook* 1996: Communicating Student Learning, pp. 90–118.

Picciotto, Linda Pierce. *Evaluation: A Team Effort*. New York: Scholastic Inc., 1992.

U.S. Department of the Interior, Office of Education. "Report Cards for Kindergarten and Elementary Grades." Leaflet 41, 1931.